WORD WORLD

Let's Use Nouns

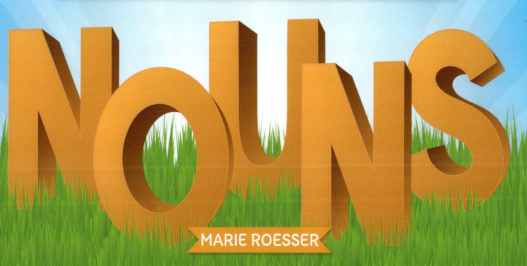

MARIE ROESSER

Please visit our website, www.enslow.com. For a free color catalog of all our high-quality books, call toll free 1-800-398-2504 or fax 1-877-980-4454.

Library of Congress Cataloging-in-Publication Data

Names: Roesser, Marie, author.
Title: Let's use nouns / Marie Roesser.
Description: New York : Enslow Publishing, [2023] | Series: Word world | Includes index.
Identifiers: LCCN 2021043676 (print) | LCCN 2021043677 (ebook) | ISBN 9781978527041 (library binding) | ISBN 9781978527027 (paperback) | ISBN 9781978527034 (set) | ISBN 9781978527058 (ebook)
Subjects: LCSH: English language--Noun--Juvenile literature. | English language--Parts of speech--Juvenile literature. | English language--Grammar--Juvenile literature.
Classification: LCC PE1201 .R64 2023 (print) | LCC PE1201 (ebook) | DDC 428.2--dc23/eng/20211122
LC record available at https://lccn.loc.gov/2021043676
LC ebook record available at https://lccn.loc.gov/2021043677

Portions of this work were originally authored by Kate Mikoley and published as *Let's Learn Nouns!*. All new material this edition authored by Marie Roesser.

First Edition
 Published in 2023 by
Enslow Publishing
29 E. 21st Street
New York, NY 10010

Copyright © 2023 Enslow Publishing

Designer: Katelyn Reynolds
Interior Layout: Rachel Rising
Editor: Therese Shea

Photo credits: Cover, pp. 2–4, 6, 8, 10, 12, 14, 16, 18, 20, 22–24 iadams/Shutterstock.com; Cover, p. 1 Faberr Ink/Shutterstock.com; Cover, p. 1 Illerlok_xolms/Shutterstock.com; Cover, p. 1 LimitedFont/Shutterstock.com; p. 5 Sylvie Bouchard/Shutterstock.com; p. 5 Daniel Kessel/Shutterstock.com; p. 5 Cumberland/Shutterstock.com; p. 5 PradaBrown/Shutterstock.com; p. 7 Ingus Kruklitis/Shutterstock.com; p. 9 Monkey Business Images/Shutterstock.com; p. 11 hyotographics/Shutterstock.com; p. 13 VGstockstudio/Shutterstock.com; p. 15 Prostock-studio/Shutterstock.com; p. 17 Chris Howey/Shutterstock.com; p. 19 Tania Kolinko/Shutterstock.com; p. 19 cheapbooks/Shutterstock.com; p. 21 Victor Shova/Shutterstock.com; p. 21 Brocreative/Shutterstock.com; p. 21 New Africa/Shutterstock.com.

All rights reserved. No part of this book may be reproduced in any form without permission in writing from the publisher, except by a reviewer.

Printed in the United States of America

Some of the images in this book illustrate individuals who are models. The depictions do not imply actual situations or events.
CPSIA compliance information: Batch #CSENS23: For further information contact Enslow Publishing, New York, New York, at 1-800-398-2504.

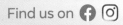

CONTENTS

Nouns Name It. 4
Common or Proper? 6
Subject or Object? 12
Many Choices 16
Concrete and Abstract. 18
More Than One 20
Glossary 22
Answer Key 22
For More Information 23
Index. 24

Words in the glossary appear in **bold** type the first time they are used in the text.

NOUNS NAME IT

How are the words *cat, school, oranges,* and *crayons* alike? They're nouns! A noun is a naming word. Nouns represent, or stand for, people, places, and things. The questions in this book will help you learn more. Check your answers on page 22.

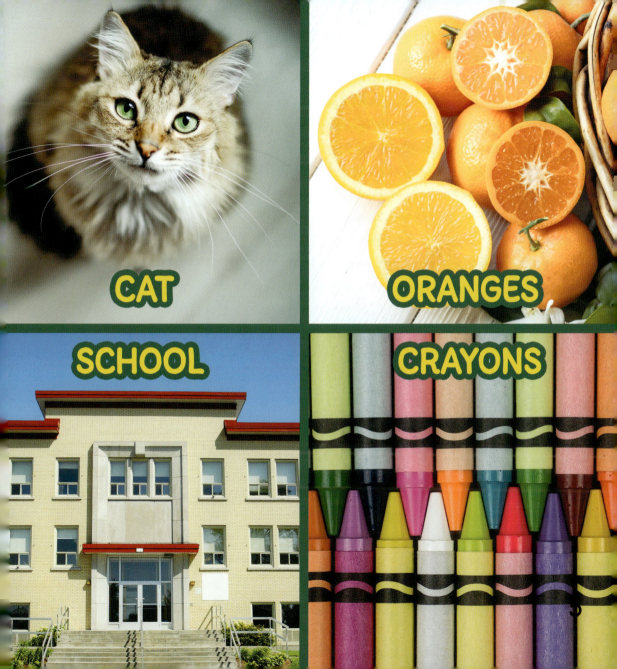

COMMON OR PROPER?

Common nouns are words for people, places, or things that aren't **specific**. *Girl* and *book* are two common nouns. They don't name which girl or which book. Read below:

This park is called Central Park.

Which is the common noun, *park* or *Central Park*?

Proper nouns are names of specific people, places, or things. What's your name? That's a proper noun! Your best friend's name is a proper noun too. Read this sentence:

Ava and her friend play basketball.

Which is the proper noun, *Ava* or *friend*?

Specific places are proper nouns too. These include the names of your school, town or city, and country. Proper nouns start with a capital letter. Common nouns usually don't. Pick out the proper nouns in this sentence:

Canada is a country in North America.

SUBJECT OR OBJECT?

A noun may be the subject of a sentence. The subject is the person, place, or thing that does the action. Let's read an example:

> The boy shares cookies.
>
> The action, or verb, is *shares*. Which noun is the subject that shares, *boy* or *cookies*?

A noun may be the object in a sentence. The object is the person, place, or thing that receives the action or is **affected** by it. Here's an example of this:

Mom drove the car.

Which noun receives or is affected by the action, *Mom* or *car*?

MANY CHOICES

Different nouns are used for the same person, place, or thing. You know that people's names are nouns. So are their jobs or other roles. Read the sentence below. Can you pick out all three nouns?

Mr. Lopez is a father and a teacher.

CONCRETE AND ABSTRACT

You **identify** some nouns with your senses. You can see, hear, touch, taste, or smell them! These are **concrete** nouns. Not all nouns are concrete. Feelings and ideas are nouns too. They're **abstract** nouns. *Love* and *time* are examples.

CONCRETE NOUNS

flower
grandmother
toy

ABSTRACT NOUNS

anger
fear
freedom

19

MORE THAN ONE

Not all nouns represent one thing. Some stand for a number of people, places, or things. For example, the nouns *team*, *family*, and *herd* represent a group. They're called collective nouns. Nouns are all around you! How many can you spot?

TEAM

FAMILY

HERD

GLOSSARY

abstract A thought or idea that isn't connected to an object.

affect To have an effect on someone or something.

concrete Having to do with certain people, places, or things rather than general ideas.

identify To find out the name or features of something.

specific Exact.

ANSWER KEY

p. 6: park

p. 8: Ava

p. 10: Canada, North America

p. 12: boy

p. 14: car

p. 16: Mr. Lopez, father, teacher

FOR MORE INFORMATION

BOOKS

Cleary, Brian P., and Jenya Prosmitsky. *A Mink, a Fink, a Skating Rink: What Is a Noun?* Minneapolis, MN: Lerner Publications, 2022.

Dahl, Michael, et al. *Nouns Say "What's That?"* North Mankato, MN: Picture Window Books, 2020.

Mahoney, Emily Jankowski. *Learn Irregular Plural Nouns with Elves.* New York, NY: Gareth Stevens Publishing, 2021.

WEBSITES

Nouns and Verbs
www.abcya.com/nouns_and_verbs.htm
Play a game to learn more about nouns and verbs.

The Noun
www.chompchomp.com/terms/noun.htm
Read more about different kinds of nouns.

What Is a Noun?
www.grammarly.com/blog/nouns/
Read about countable nouns and possessive nouns.

Publisher's note to educators and parents: Our editors have carefully reviewed these websites to ensure that they are suitable for students. Many websites change frequently, however, and we cannot guarantee that a site's future contents will continue to meet our high standards of quality and educational value. Be advised that students should be closely supervised whenever they access the internet.

INDEX

abstract nouns, 18, 19

actions, 12, 14

capital letters, 10

collective nouns, 20

common nouns, 6, 10

concrete nouns, 18, 19

naming, 4

object, 14

proper nouns, 8, 10

subject, 12